QUEEN ELIZABETH
The Queen Mother

COOMBE BOOKS

Ever since she entered the public arena with her marriage to Prince Albert, King George V's second son, Queen Elizabeth the Queen Mother has charmed the nation and won its undying affection. She, perhaps more than any other member of the Royal Family this century, has added a sense of warmth and approachability to an institution that confounds its critics by enduring and indeed gaining in popularity.

Her happy home life, as the youngest daughter in a family of ten children, can hardly have prepared her for the onerous duties as Queen Consort when her husband so suddenly acceded to the Throne on the abdication of his brother. Yet it is a role that she managed to carry out with charm, grace and considerable skill.

Born, as so often stated, 'with the century,' Elizabeth Bowes-Lyon, daughter of the 14th Earl of Strathmore and Kinghorne, was educated at home under the guidance of her governess, Mrs Clara Cooper Knight and the watchful eye of her mother.

The seemingly interminable years of the First World War were spent at the family's ancestral home: Glamis Castle, in Scotland, where the youthful Elizabeth played a modest yet, to the soldiers in her 'care', important part in the war.

With the end of hostilities, the London Season witnessed her presentation to the King and Queen as a *débutante,* and her presence was constantly requested at an endless succession of glittering society events.

It was on one such occasion – a dance held at the London home of Lady Farquhar in 1920 – that she was to catch the eye of the normally retiring Prince Albert. The ensuing courtship, of which the suitor's parents were kept informed, flourished and in 1921 Prince Albert, now the Duke of York, asked for Elizabeth's hand in marriage. The proposal was turned down. Undeterred by the refusal, however, Albert, after a respectful period, was to take up the cause once more and his second proposal, in January 1923, was accepted.

The wedding ceremony, just three months later, was as splendid as it was historic, for it was the first time in over 650 years that a male member of the Royal Family was married in Westminster Abbey.

Commoner she may have been, but the reception the new Duchess of York was given by the crowds that lined London's streets that day was nothing short of regal. The people, as well as the Royal Family itself, had taken the bride to their hearts, and she in turn would reward them with the unassuming graciousness that was to become her hallmark.

On their return from honeymoon, the newlyweds made White Lodge in Richmond Park their London base, although royal duties were to keep them away from their home for extended periods.

The birth of Princess Elizabeth in 1926 put a temporary halt to the Duchess' varied duties, but just nine months later they were off again, this time on their only official tour as Duke and Duchess of York – to Australia and New Zealand.

In 1936 the happiness of the family's home life was shattered by the death of the ailing King and the subsequent abdication of his successor: the uncrowned Edward VIII. His long-standing friendship with Wallis Simpson was well known, but the decision to relinquish the Crown was totally unexpected and put an almost unbearable burden on the shoulders of his younger brother.

The Accession of George VI to the Throne brought with it new and increased responsibilities; ones that both the new King and his Consort were to accept and carry out with a single-minded dedication that was typical of their reign.

Throughout the war, the King and Queen remained among their people, living for much of the time in a bomb-damaged Buckingham Palace and enduring some of the hardships that others throughout the country had to face. They continued to carry out many of their formal duties and took on the additional task of bolstering the spirit of the Nation at this critical moment in its history. It is a contribution that the people will never forget.

The public's gratitude to, and affection for, the Monarchy was amply expressed during the victory celebrations and the Silver Wedding festivities that followed the war – if ever the King and Queen had doubted the devotion of their subjects, all such thoughts must have been dispelled by the displays of loyalty that the events engendered.

The death of George VI in 1952, although not altogether unexpected considering his frail state of health, was a severe blow to the devoted and loving wife. However, the Queen Mother did not allow herself the luxury of a protracted public mourning, and although she became rather withdrawn in private, her inner strength, as well as the support of family and friends, saw her through this difficult period. Unlike some of her illustrious predecessors, the Queen Mother was to pick up the pieces of her life and accept the challenges of her position with renewed vigour and commitment.

Now in her eighty-third year, the Queen Mother shoulders her share of the royal workload unflinchingly, although, in deference to her age, this is now somewhat reduced.

As a private person, the Queen Mother maintains her keen interest in the Arts and outdoor life. She takes great pride and pleasure in her growing family, which now numbers six grandchildren and three great-grandchildren, and continues to enjoy the love and esteem of a grateful Nation.

The Queen Mother and relatives at Badminton, April 1982. Her youngest grandson Prince Edward escorted her to Badminton church on the final day (below) while the Duchess of Beaufort emerged with the Queen Mother after the service (right).

"All's well that ends well" might well be the family motto for the Queen Mother's long and distinguished line of ancestors. Like most noble families whose histories have been inextricably bound up with national politics and aristocratic machination, hers can boast a pretty rollicking ancestry, though it has borne its share of defeat and disgrace amid its record of success, honour and respect. Willie Hamilton, the Member of Parliament most frequently denounced as the thorn in the

well (possibly, for records are by no means precise) as his knighthood. His great-grandson Patrick became a Peer of the Scottish Parliament and was created the first Lord Glamis in 1445, the date from which the succession of the family's aristocratic titles begins. There was a desultory but bloody period of intense royal disfavour when King James V conceived that the Glamis family were involved in plotting against him. Both John, seventh Lord Glamis, and his brother George

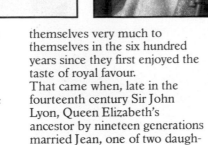

side of the monarchy's flesh, has described the Queen Mother's ancestry as "poorish by aristocratic standards," and whatever this may mean in his own jaundiced and often abusive mind, it is true that her forefathers have until comparatively recently kept

themselves very much to themselves in the six hundred years since they first enjoyed the taste of royal favour.
That came when, late in the fourteenth century Sir John Lyon, Queen Elizabeth's ancestor by nineteen generations married Jean, one of two daugh-

ters of Robert II, King of Scotland and grandson of the famous Robert the Bruce. Shortly beforehand, Sir John had been granted the thanage of Glamis after several years of royal service, and his marriage brought him additional lands in the form of nearby Tannadyce as

were imprisoned by him while, by sheer coincidence, the widow of the sixth Baron Bowes, an ancestress on the other side of the family, was burnt as a witch in 1537 after having also been accused of designs against the King. Elsewhere in the family, beheadings, deaths while escaping royal custody, and wholesale forfeiture of lands seemed to tumble over one another with monotonous regularity, but with the death of James V and the accession of Mary Queen of Scots, the Strathmore, and its members entered into a long period of grace with Britain's monarchy. Real, fluid prosperity, however, did not arrive until the middle of the 18th century, when the ninth Earl married Eleanor Bowes, the

who survived secured their release from prison and the repossession of property. Better times were ushered in with the accession of James VI as James I of England in 1603: Patrick, the ninth Lord Glamis, was made a Privy Councillor and given the title of Earl of Kinghorne. Despite some embarrassing family support for the anti-Catholic League of the Covenant in the years that followed, and an even more embarrassing debt of £400,000 which the third Earl inherited and could only liquidate by a life of "frugality and prudence," the family's title was extended within two more generations to include

only child of a wealthy industrialist from County Durham. His estates covered much of the county, parts of Yorkshire and land in Hertfordshire, and he almost gladly transferred them to the Lyon family on condition that they changed their name to Bowes. This strange *quid pro quo*,

The wedding of Mr Nicholas Soames, grandson of Sir Winston Churchill, to Miss Catherine Weatherall provided another opportunity for a family outing. The Queen Mother took Princess Margaret, the Prince of Wales and Lady Diana Spencer to the service, held at St Margaret's Church Westminster in May 1981.

the perverse result of greed and snobbery by today's standards, but entirely justifiable in the context of the hard realities of contemporary aristocratic life at the crossroads of the industrial revolution, was agreed to without much demur, though when the old man died, the Earl did a partial *volte-face* and combined both names in the family name of Lyon-Bowes. A century later the 13th Earl, the Queen Mother's grandfather, redressed the balance somewhat by calling himself Bowes-Lyon

virtues of sewing and shopping, and showed an early liking, if not exactly an expertise, for horse-riding – a pastime which was not to last beyond adolescence.
As a teenager she used to spend the winters with each of her two grandmothers who lived on the French and Italian Rivieras. These holidays gave her the opportunity to supplement her French conversation, learned from whom her brother called "a succession of French governesses," to the degree of fluency which has characterised her delivery ever since. She also developed a precocious talent for gardening, turning her meagre 6 x 12 feet plot at Glamis into a triumph of colour with a succession of polyanthus, roses and grape-hyacinth. David

and there, with a coat of arms quartered by bows and lions to prove it, it has remained ever since.

Time invariably invests a half-forgotten age with the golden tinge of vague nostalgia, and an Edwardian childhood in the immutable world of the aristocracy before the lamps went out is as liable to this indulgence as any. Queen Elizabeth herself, in a 1948 broadcast, referred to her upbringing as "my own happy childhood," and there is indeed a general consensus that no place, event or personality of those early years clouded the infant mind. Lady Elizabeth was, according to her nurse, "an exceptionally happy, easy baby,

crawling early, running at thirteen months and speaking very young;" and she was soon the adored, and perhaps a little indulged, baby of a family whose way of life was bright, playful and loving. She learned Bible story after Bible story at her mother's knee, showed a penchant for flowers, and a love of parties and children's games. As a pupil she was questioning and adept, if a little mischievous; she enjoyed the housewifely

shared her enjoyment of the outdoor world – he himself was to become an authority on trees and shrubs, gardening and landscaping – and it was with him that Lady Elizabeth, walking among Scotland's moorland heathers or fishing in her lakes and rivers, spent the long, late summers of a dying era.

She could not fail to remember the day which signified its end. It was August 4th 1914, a Bank holiday and, more to the point, her fourteenth birthday, and she celebrated it with a visit to London's Coliseum Theatre where the family had rented a box. At some time during the

long variety performance which she had gone to watch the news broke, perhaps unofficially, to end the month-old speculation on the likelihood of war, and the theatre buzzed with rumours. At the end of the show she emerged into streets she described as "filled with people shouting and full of enthusiasm," as Londoners, fervently patriotic and tragically unsuspecting of its consequences, hailed the beginning of the European conflict with prolonged and rousing cheers. As she lay in bed that night Lady Elizabeth could hear the swell of voices as the entire capital, it seemed, flocked up the Mall to Buckingham Palace to acclaim the man who, less than nine years later, would be her father-in-law.

The London Season habit was not slow in returning after the cessation of hostilities, even though the uncertain and self-conscious resumption of

everyday life muted the brilliance of the palmier pre-War days, and the youngest of the Strathmore girls now took full advantage. She returned to London for the great occasions, such as Royal Ascot and, in July, the national Victory March, and for the more relaxed social enjoyments like parties, receptions and society weddings. It was the year of her social *début,* her "coming-out," and like all *débutantes* of high birth, she was presented to the King and Queen at Court. There followed a succession of invitations to dances, where she immediately won a string of admirers and was

Elizabeth. But Prince Albert, now Duke of York, was only temporarily put off and began to see her again in the spring. It seems that later that year, and probably as a result of the frequent references that the Duke made to Lady Elizabeth in his letters to his mother, Queen Mary and her newly-married daughter paid their respects to the Strathmores at Glamis, and towards the end of 1922 the Duke was there again, preparing the way for his next attempt at winning the lady he had wooed for two years. Early in the New Year the Strathmores came down to London and on the

generally agreed to be the most accompanied dancer in London. The charming young dancer first met her future husband, then Prince Albert, at a dance in May 1920. She made such an impression upon the shy prince that he was driven to court her persistently and to the exclusion of all others for two and a half years. The first proposal of marriage, in the autumn of 1921, was turned down by Lady

Britain and the Commonwealth paid enthusiastic tributes to the Queen Mother amid celebrations to mark her 80th birthday. On 15th July, some three weeks in advance, London was the scene of colourful processions as the Royal Family, including Princess Alice and the Duchess of Gloucester (far left), Princess Anne, Princess Margaret, Lady Sarah Armstrong-Jones (above left), and the Queen, Prince Philip and Prince Edward (above) attended a thanksgiving service in St Paul's Cathedral. The Archbishop of Canterbury delivered a moving and appreciative address ending with the words "Thank you, Your Majesty. Thanks be to God". Crowds swarmed round Buckingham Palace to acclaim the Queen Mother when she appeared on the balcony afterwards.

weekend of 12th and 13th January invited the Duke to stay at St Paul's Walden Bury. Both families knew what to expect from this visit and before leaving for Hertfordshire the Duke told his parents that he would telegraph a message to them at Sandringham as soon as he had news for them. On Sunday 13th, the Duke and Lady Elizabeth excused themselves from church – a request that seems to have been granted without the need for explanation – and went for a walk together in the woods which had once been the lady's childhood hideaway. Here the Duke made his second, and successful, proposal of marriage and soon afterwards a telegram

announcing simply "Alright, Bertie" was flashed to the Norfolk countryside, to add a rare touch of magic to the repetitive royal way of life hallowed as immutable for a Sandringham January.

By contrast to what has often been suspected in subsequent royal romances, no delay was allowed between the granting of parental consents and the public announcement of the *fait accompli*. The Court Circular recorded the royal engagement with its one customary, heavily-formulated sentence on 16th January and the evening papers and the following day's nationals brimmed with the triumph and congratulation of it all.

Racing, the sport of kings, is a long-popular sport with the Royal Family. The Queen Mother is a noted owner of steeplechasers and is one of the most successful in the country. Her eldest daughter, Queen Elizabeth, on the other hand, is more interested in the Flat. As a result the annual royal outing to Ascot (facing page in 1981) is of more immediate interest to the Queen, but the Queen Mother seems to enjoy the visits as much as anyone. (Overleaf) the racing at Ascot in 1983 provided the Royal Family with hours of fun and enjoyment, beginning with the Royal Procession along the course.

Headlines ran across full pages, torrents of sub-heads summarising incidental details cascaded down double columns, historians came forth to contribute articles on Lady Elizabeth's ancestry and

After her engagement to Prince Charles, the now Princess of Wales was seen more and more in the company of the Queen Mother. (This page) at Ascot in 1981, as Lady Diana, and (facing page) at Braemar in 1982.

biography, gossip writers on the ladies' pages fairly weakened at the knees. For a day at least, Mayfair society was indistinguishable from any other community in the country in the intensity of interest over the forthcoming marriage, and Lady Elizabeth was mildly taken aback by it. "We hoped we were going to get a few days' peace," she wrote to a friend. "But the cat is now completely out of the bag and there is no possibility of stuffing him back. I feel very happy but quite dazed." Indeed, no-one seemed other than happy, if a little dazed. The Earl and Countess of Strathmore came to Sandringham with their daughter the following weekend

where they saw the King, Queen and the 78-year-old Queen Alexandra as well as the Duke of York. His parents were delighted with the prospective daughter-in-law: the King found her "pretty and charming," the Queen additionally thought she was "so . . . engaging and natural." Both testified to their son's supreme happiness. Everyone, it seemed, was happy. As if by universal consent to the unwritten code which dictates that the more hopeless the human condition the more readily must any opportunity for diversion be seized, the whole nation, still in the grip of economic recession following a temporary and artificial post-War

On 1st August, 1979, the Queen Mother became the first woman to be installed as Lord Warden of the Cinque Ports, in succession to Sir Robert Menzies, former Prime Minister of Australia. The installation ceremony took place at Dover, and thousands of people turned out to watch the spectacle as the Queen Mother left Dover Castle in procession (bottom left), inspected guards of honour drawn from the Army (right) and the Navy (below right), and received flowers from the local children during her walkabout (bottom centre). (Facing page) after her 83rd birthday.

boom, looked forward eagerly to the coming theatre of royal romance.

By contrast the time-honoured rituals were being played out. On 12th February a special meeting of the Privy Council was called to give formal consent, under the Royal Marriages Act of 1772, to the Duke of York's wedding, and a clerk then spent three days and almost two dozen quill pens setting out, in illuminated manuscript on parchment, the terms of the Marriage Licence.

McVitie & Price of Edinburgh were commissioned to bake the wedding cake, and plans went ahead for London to be decked out as never before, with heavy bunting strung across roads, entwined A's and E's everywhere and three miles of illuminations through the streets of the West End. In a gesture which was to be repeated at subsequent royal weddings, special facilities for incapacitated ex-servicemen to witness the processions at Buckingham Palace were arranged – a tactful and considerate concession by a family who knew its debt to millions of war dead and wounded. Less publicised preparations – the design and manufacture of the bride's wedding dress and trousseau – were accompanied by advice and speculation in the papers and magazines of the day as to their final outcome. *Punch* modified its habitual deference with a touch

In February 1982 the Queen Mother visited Canada House. After a brief conversation with the High Commissioner, Mrs Jean Wadds (far left), she declared a new Cultural Centre open to the public. There was a faint hint of mischief in the Queen Mother's eye (this page) when, in May 1983, she visited Smithfield Market and became the target of good-natured lèse-majesté at the hands of its stall-holders. Interspersed among the formalities of her tour were spontaneous acts of gallantry from meat cutters, porters and packers as they seized her hands and kissed them, and serenaded her with patriotic songs.

of respectable humour: it quoted an American newspaper which had erroneously referred to the bridegroom as the Duke of New York, and concluded that the mistake was understandable since after all the Duke was "about to enter the united state." The passing of Easter and the promise of Spring intensified the anticipation of Lady Elizabeth's wedding and huge crowds were expected to turn out onto the processional route. A Mrs Sykes of Walthamstow was the first person known to have taken up her position, shortly after midnight on 26th April: she was something of a character, having

The Order of the Garter is, unlike so many other honours, the personal gift of the sovereign and is only awarded on her express instructions. In 1936, King George VI made his wife a Lady of the Garter just three days after his accession. The Queen Mother has continued to attend the annual service of the Order at Windsor ever since. The history of the Order dates back to the fourteenth century when King Edward III retrieved a lady's garter which had slipped off during a dance. Noticing his smirking courtiers the King remarked "Honi soit qui mal y pense", evil be to he that evil thinks, and founded the Order with that same motto.

performed a similar ritual for Princess Mary's wedding fourteen months earlier. By two o'clock a few small gatherings had formed; four hours later the routes were lined, and hawkers of white heather, capitalising out of the bride's Scottish origins, began to do a roaring trade. Seats began to be taken in the Abbey at 9.30 and by ten o'clock, with an hour and a half to go, several parts of the route were seven-deep with people and there were six thousand people outside No. 17 Bruton Street, the unpretentious Victorian house which had been Lord and Lady Strathmore's London home since 1919 and from which the bride would leave for her wedding.

Albert Duke of York was almost five years older than his twenty-two-year old wife, though if the age difference appears wide it was nothing to the contrast in their respective upbringings.

Whereas hers was secure, loving, familial, his was formal, cold and unbelievably restricted. His parents, dutiful royalties though they undoubtedly were, lacked any natural parental instinct save the satisfaction of having done what was expected of them in producing children at all, and a distant pride in the limited achievements of their off-spring as they grew up. Over-impressed by the awe-inspiring dignity and

Pastel shades have always been closely associated with the Queen Mother. This, together with her penchant for feathers, was confirmed at her installation as Warden of the Cinque Ports in 1979 (opposite, top right) and at many subsequent events.

unbending traditions of the later years of Queen Victoria's court, they maintained that aura of majesty and unflinching obligation throughout the more urbane years of Edward VII, and reinstated it on their own accession in 1910. Their reign had already seen the restoration of several ancient ceremonies, including the Investiture of the Prince of Wales and many refinements to Trooping the Colour, which had become almost atrophied through lack of use. By the end of World War I, in which their sense of duty twice resulted in an excess of patriotic zeal – the Palace ban on alcohol failed to catch on and the Proclamation of July 1917, by which the family and dynasty name became Windsor – they had established their style so effectively that even in the liberated, adventurous

atmosphere of the 1920s no-one questioned the one British institution which growing egalitarianism should logically have begun to affect.

All this, and its aftermath which culminated in the glorious success of the Silver Jubilee of 1935, was achieved at great cost to the King and Queen's children. Freda Dudley-Ward opined that King George V "considered them dolts, the lot of them," and Prince Albert, known in what appears to be one of the few informal parental gestures ever thrown his way as Bertie, probably got the worst of every bargain. As if in grim portent of his future, he was born on the worst possible day – 14th December, the day on

which the Prince Consort in 1861, and Queen Victoria's gifted daughter Princess Alice in 1878, died and the old Queen's dread of that sorrowful anniversary was fast in the process of growing mightier by the year. Placated though she eventually was, Prince Albert, who was never a strong child, suffered from continued stomach disorders and other more common ailments and the treatment meted out by one of his earlier nurses, which included bottle-feeding while on bumpy rides in carriages, is said to have rooted his life-long difficulties over his digestion. He was also fearfully nervous, much of which may have been due to his father's irascible chaffing and his mother's

After a conversation with Lord Mildmay in 1949, the Queen Mother took to steeplechasing with great enthusiasm. This interest has continued ever since and the Queen Mother is now credited with over three hundred winners. (Overleaf) the Queen Mother accompanied many members of her family to Ascot in 1983.

uncomfortably remote attitude with him, and by early childhood he was already cursed with a stammer that to one degree or another was to dog his verbal delivery throughout his life. His condition, physical and psychological, was not improved by the almost obligatory process of naval training at Dartmouth, and although he showed enthusiasm his powers of learning were far from excellent, and the constant derision he received at the hands of his fellow cadets tortured him. Eventually he served in the Great War, and saw action at

Jutland but all that, like much of his naval career, was constantly interrupted and eventually curtailed by his persistent poor health.

In many ways it seems remarkable that he had the psychological resilience to pursue his bride through a courtship of over two years, yet one feels instinctly that much of his persistence was born of the desperate need to release himself not only from his own family and parents but from the monotonous and possibly degrading dependence upon them which continued bachelorhood entailed. He was absolutely right to imagine that

his life style was long overdue for a completely new dimension and when, shortly after his wedding, he received a letter from his father which stated that, "I am quite certain that Elizabeth will be a splendid partner in your work and share with you and help you in all you have to do," he probably read more into its significance for him than the writer had ever intended.

In the first days of 1936 the much loved and well-respected monarch, King George V, died. Upon his death his popular eldest son came to the throne as

King Edward VIII, but even as he ascended the throne the storm clouds which would destroy him were gathering. There can be little doubt that the name of Wallis Simpson was too often mentioned in London Society for it to be unknown to members of the Royal Family, nor that the lady's ready fame owed everything to her popularity with the new King. As Prince of Wales, he had met her at a country house in Leicestershire five years before and, following his usual penchant for married women, had formed a barely concealed but, in the quaint and rather hypocritical circumstances in

the problem remained unspoken of until, months after the parent's demise, it began to surface beyond further concealment. By October 1936, all those most closely concerned were in no doubt that the King wished to marry his constant companion and that, it was constitutionally impossible for her, twice divorced – as by the end of that month she was – and with both husbands living, to be crowned consort to a King pledged to defend a faith which abhorred and shunned divorce. It is unlikely that the Duchess of York envisaged anything remotely approaching her brother-in-law's abdication

which high society then functioned, respectable liaison. There is evidence that King George V knew of it and feared the inevitable development into a prospect of marriage and its potential for creating trouble, and both he and his heir harboured independent intentions to discuss the matter together. For various reasons, eminently understandable in the light of their uncertain and almost distrustful relationship,

when, in the Spring of 1936, she and the Duke visited him, at Fort Belvedere – the visit would otherwise almost certainly not have taken place particularly as one of the King's guests at the time was Mrs Simpson herself. This is the first recorded encounter between the two future sisters-in-law and there was suspicion from the start: Mrs Simpson noticed, with her usual ready perception, that the Duchess "was not sold" on the

Mid-May 1982 found the Queen Mother in Paris, visiting France once again as she has, on and off, since her teens. This particular visit was part private, part official, the main purpose being to open a new wing of the Hertford British Hospital, on 12th May – the 45th anniversary of her Coronation. That afternoon, she took tea with President Mitterand who accompanied Her Majesty to the main entrance of the Elysée Palace (these pages) on her departure. Having visited France officially five times in the previous quarter of a century, and on many other private occasions, the Queen Mother knows the Bordeaux region and the Chateaux of the Loire well. It is said that she influenced the decision to send Princess Anne for a stay in France in the early-1960s.

King's "American interest." The hour-long meeting was not followed up until early that July when the new King gave a dinner party at York House, St. James's Palace, where both Mrs Simpson and the Yorks were amongst the guests. Again, what contact occurred was cool and it is generally reckoned to be consequent upon this event that mutual dislike between the two ladies germinated. Matters were not improved by the knowledge that Mrs Simpson was acting as hostess during the King's stay at Balmoral where he busied himself entertaining society friends on a grand scale – this to the consternation of Queen Mary, who was much put out by the conspicuous absence, for want of royal invitation, of the usual Establishment figures – nor by several other examples of the King's waywardness, the most famous being the cancellation of an official engagement in Aberdeen, ostensibly on grounds of mourning, but in reality affording the opportunity for him to greet Mrs Simpson personally after her long train journey to Balmoral.

By all accounts, and understandably, it was a time of profound shock. With Queen Mary still grieving in early widowhood and dependent upon the support of her only daughter the Princess Royal, and with the Duke of York shattered under the mounting pressure of an inexorable destiny, it fell to the Duchess to lead the prolonged and, in events, hopeless attack against the King. The play *Crown Matrimonial* which enjoyed a lengthy success on the stage and television in the mid 1970s cast the Duchess as the dominant adversary to King Edward, berating him for his lack of judgement, the inept handling of the issue and, above all, for keeping all his family so totally uninformed. That last score at least is well supported by evidence. Like her husband, the Duchess of York was angered at the seemingly systematic way in which the King avoided all attempts to be contacted by his brother until most of the vital decisions had effectively been made. The Duke of York finally forced a meeting, but not before the Duchess, blazing with frustration, had complained, "Everyone knows more than we do. We know nothing! Nothing!"

In the meantime she, like her royal relations had to cope with her usual round of public

engagements and, domestically, with the natural inquisitiveness of her two children. To them and to members of her retinue she maintained an outward air of wistful resignation: "We must take what's coming to us, and make the best of it," she told Miss Crawford, the Princesses' governess. On other occasions her indignation bordered on contempt: before the year was out she affirmed bitterly, "None of this would have happened if Wallis hadn't blown in from Baltimore!"

By the early afternoon of 11th December 1936 everything *had* happened. Parliament gave effect to the Abdication Act, and in giving the Royal Assent to it, King Edward VIII ceased to be an Empire's sovereign. He was

On 13th April, 1982, the Queen Mother attended a gala concert by the Royal Philharmonic Orchestra, of which she is patron. Also taking part was the great opera singer, Luciano Pavarotti. After the show the Queen Mother was charmed by Pavarotti's gallant gesture (far right). (Opposite page) the Queen Mother wearing two of her favourite tiaras.

even then preparing his final broadcast to the nation before leaving for France. In his place, by automatic succession, the Duke of York assumed the throne and his Duchess, now Queen, entered the Litany of the Church of England for the first time. Perversely she was laid low with influenza at 145 Piccadilly, ending the year much as she had started it, and she was unable to be present as the Royal Family bid tearful, incredulous farewells to the departing ex-King at Windsor. Instead, she sent him a letter, which he read in the car which took him to Portsmouth Dockyard. Despite the past weeks' bitterness, its contents were probably devoid of unfair

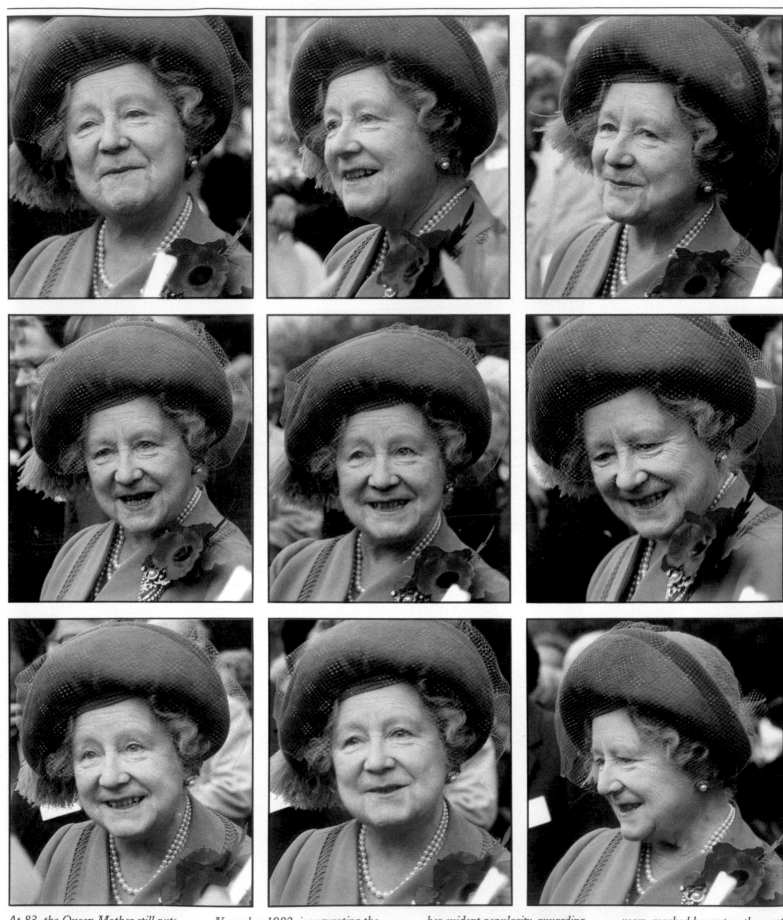

At 83, the Queen Mother still puts everything into her public appearances. At Hyde Park in November 1982, inaugurating the Beautiful Britain campaign she was as animated as ever, revelling in her evident popularity, rewarding it with the concern, kindness and sheer fun which have, for sixty years, marked her out as the most lovable member of the Royal Family.

reproach: the character of the writer suggests the possibility; the kindly message "Hope Elizabeth better" in the exile's first telegram from France the following morning seems to clinch it.

Considering the immediate aftermath of the Abdication it would be almost facile to state that the new Queen harboured no illusions about the task that lay ahead. Melbourne may have admired the quiet courage of the eighteen-year-old Queen Victoria as she assumed a discredited Throne, and Churchill was later to romanticise the vision of a young charming Queen following her well-loved father in 1952, but the maturer years of the King and Queen in December 1936 were no bar to public admiration. The archangel who would, according to Macaulay, have shrunk from

In July 1982, the Queen Mother toured the sailing barge Dannebrog *at St Katherine's Dock in London. This craft is the team base of the Operation Drake Fellowship which, inaugurated under Prince Charles' auspices in the 1970s, offers training courses to unemployed school-leavers in Britain's urban areas. Another link with her grandson came the Queen Mother's way on 28th October, 1982, when she attended a reception at the Press Club to commemorate its centenary (opposite page). While there she unveiled a portrait of her grandson, the Prince of Wales, who is the Club's patron. (Overleaf) The Queen Mother with her family at Ascot in 1983.*

the prospect of Victoria's destiny in 1837 would have viewed the implications of the unexpected accession almost a century later with equal or greater distaste. No sooner was the new monarch crowned than the threat of war began to spread across Europe. Hitler's ambitions and ruthlessness were becoming clear while statesmen tried to appease him in a vain attempt to avoid the horrors of war.

When war finally came, at 11 o'clock on Sunday 3rd September, the Queen was still at Balmoral with the two Princesses. She came down South to join the King

immediately, leaving her daughters to complete as much as possible of what would be their last proper summer holiday at Queen Victoria's famous Highland retreat.

Winston Churchill was later to rhapsodise somewhat fulsomely over the effect the Queen had upon her husband's subjects on these sometimes depressing tours – "Many an aching heart found solace in her gracious smile" – but in the context of

the heavy protocol which had for most of the century tended to distance the Crown from its people, the royal progresses offered a welcome glimmer of hope and even purpose during those painfully desperate early war years. Nor were they isolated examples of the Queen's concern for Britain's spiritual uplift. She made full and frequent use of the radio, using the precedents set by George V and particularly Edward VIII to drive home messages of encouragement to housewives, those who played surrogate parents to evacuated children, nurses and medical volunteers. She stressed the importance of maintaining the family unit while home life was under pressure: "We must see to it," she told the women of Britain in 1940, "that our homes do not lose those

(These pages) though she often has to wrap up (above centre and top left), the Queen Mother always attends Badminton. Other equestrian events also figure strongly in her calendar. (Overleaf) special cheers greeted the Queen Mother at the wedding of the Prince of Wales and Lady Diana Spencer at St Paul's Cathedral in 1981. Escorted by Prince Edward to the service and by Prince Andrew for the return journey, she looked thrilled with the splendour and pageantry of it all. As the bride and groom walked down the aisle a broad beam of delight lit up her face, though she had dabbed away the occasional tear during the more solemn moments of the marriage service.

very qualities which make them the background, as well as the joy of our lives." She also broadcast a message, in French, to the women of occupied France in 1940, and she did not forget the importance of American assistance, crucial even before the United States entered the war the following year. In a radio appeal to the women of America for continuing help in the hour of crisis, the Queen said, "To us in the time of tribulation you have surely shown the compassion which has for two thousand years been the mark of the good neighbour."

The British Royal House, like most of the constitutional monarchies of Europe with the exception of Belgium, came through the War and its whirlwind aftermath dominated by the Soviet push from the East, not only unscathed but strengthened. It must have been with utter dismay that the King and Queen saw their distant relatives and fellow monarchs liquidated or bundled out of their eastern European lands as Roumania, Bulgaria and Yugoslavia fell to Communist republicanism just as in 1918 Austria, Prussia and Russia had collapsed under the weight of humiliating defeats at the hands of their adversaries. In Greece the monarchy, which had never in the previous quarter century

been sufficiently stable to increase its chances of survival, swayed this way and that at the mercy of politicians of the left and right, and the Italians wasted little time ridding themselves of King Victor Emmanuel III and his son of short reign, Umberto II.
But as the remaining western European monarchs returned from exile to their homelands, the British Royal Family were able to command the spontaneous affection and loyalty of the surging masses who surrounded Buckingham Palace, for having been with them throughout the worst bombing and the privations of this most cataclysmic of wars. The Queen even received a poem from a lady in Chicago, praising her for "wearing your gayest gown, your bravest smile . . . when London Bridge was burning down," and Eleanor Roosevelt, ever the most dispassionate of commentators, averred that "in all my contacts with them I have gained the greatest respect for the King and Queen. Both of them are doing an extraordinarily outstanding job for the people. You admire their character and devotion to duty." Little wonder therefore, that the King and Queen found themselves the objects of such

great tribute on the many occasions when the victory was celebrated. In nine of the most challenging years, particularly for sovereigns of such little previous first-hand experience, they had triumphed – and all by their own efforts.
It was all the more unfair, therefore, that the royal couple would not be able to relax and enjoy their achievements. The King's health began to fail; first there was circulatory trouble, which almost led to gangrene, then a malignant growth in the lung. At times the King seemed to rally, but the deterioration was all too clear. His Queen, however, kept her public composure, even when she and the King walked out onto the

An informal outdoor royal birthday gathering to which all were welcome: these two youngsters (top) were among the hundreds of people who waited for a glimpse of the Queen Mother outside Clarence House (above) on the morning of her 82nd birthday, just before attending Prince William's christening. Predictably the single marigold was as acceptable as any official bouquet. A single rose, too, (left) for the Queen Mother during her 1982 visit to London Gardens – she is most at home against this backdrop of well-tended, colourful blooms in natural settings (opposite page).

tarmac at Heathrow airport to bid farewell to Princess Elizabeth as she and her husband left on a Commonwealth tour.

But she knew, and the pitifully preoccupied look on the King's face made it clear that he knew too, that this would be his last sight of his daughter. It was a cold and windy day, and the King, gaunt, staring, swamped in a heavy great-coat yet bare-

The christening of Prince William at Buckingham Palace meant more to the Queen Mother than a great family occasion: it focused upon the unsuspecting child born to be the eventual successor to her husband – his great-grandfather King George VI. Prince Charles was canny enough to mark a further significance – the link between Prince William's birth and the Victorian era – by choosing the Queen Mother's 82nd birthday for the christening.

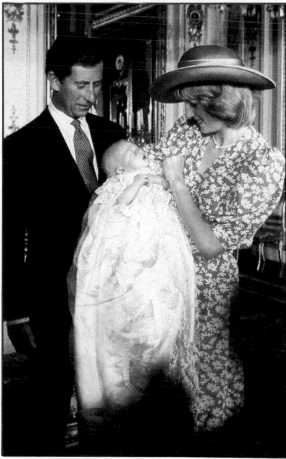

headed, strained for a last lingering look of the departing Argonaut aircraft. Then he made his leaden-hearted way back to Buckingham Palace, and thence eventually to Sandringham. It was there that he spent 5th February shooting hares at Flitcham, on the Sandringham Estate, while the Queen and Princess Margaret motored across Norfolk for a cruise on the Broads and a visit to the

Royal Ascot is another of the Queen Mother's annual magnets, and while she is no fashion extrovert, she enjoys the opportunity to wear some of her colourful summery outfits. The daily order of royal processions changes as different members of her family join the festival: (this page) with the Queen in 1982; (opposite page) with the Queen and Lady Diana Spencer in 1981, and with Princess Margaret in 1982.

painter Edward Seago, joining the King back at the Big House that evening. And it was there too that in the small hours of the following day he died, discovered at daybreak by his valet who had brought his early morning tea.

Clarence House and Queen Elizabeth the Queen Mother have become almost synonymous in the last thirty years, just as Marlborough House had been with Queen Mary. It is in fact part of St James's Palace, which it effectively adjoins, and has been described – in a rather vain attempt to make it sound remotely comparable to anything in the more common run of houses – as two back-to-back houses joined into one. It was built by John Nash for King William IV when he was Duke of Clarence, in 1825, almost forty years after he had first occupied a house on the same site. Queen Victoria's mother had lived there for twenty years, and it eventually became the home – though not much lived in – of Arthur, Duke of Connaught until his death, as Queen Victoria's last surviving son, in 1942. After serving as a Red Cross headquarters for five years, it was taken over in 1949 and much modernised, as White Lodge had been in its day, by Princess Elizabeth and the Duke of Edinburgh, whose second child Princess Anne was born there in August 1950. The Queen Mother has succeeded, as no other royal occupant this century, in making it the perfect permanent London home. Although it houses administrative offices, and despite the noble display of royal insignia outside – even the lamp-posts are surmounted by

miniature crowns – its cream-painted exterior and heavy, highly-polished mahogany doors enclose a spacious, restful house which in design, furnishing and ornamentation is *very* Queen Mother. A plethora of silver trophies chart her satisfyingly successful thirty-five-year old career as a race-horse owner; glass-fronted cabinets house her collection of Red Anchor period Chelsea china, accumulated over many years; her weakness for Regency wine coasters is revealed, and the huge mirrors and chandeliers, the heavy velvet drapes and valances at the windows add luxurious style to this otherwise homely building.

Her private sitting-room sports a marble mantlepiece built, before the house itself, in the mid-18th century, but the Queen Mother's taste for the more modern expressions of art are epitomised by the wide variety of pictures she has collected: Sickert, the English impressionist, she is very fond of; L.S. Lowry she discovered before most other people did; Edward Seago is well patronised by the Royal Family, and all have a place here. Alongside are such occasional paintings as a portrait of King George VI investing Princess

There is arguably no subject nearer to the Queen Mother's heart, nor more readily identified with her than that of the garden.

Her patronage of the London Gardens Society is now long established, and marked by her annual tours of prize-winning

gardens in various parts of the capital. On 14th July, 1982, she visited gardens in Kensington and Wandsworth (these pages), casting

an expert eye (top centre) as she wandered through allées, engaging in erudite horticultural conversation with her hosts.

Elizabeth with the Order of the Garter, and an uncompleted portrait of the Queen Mother herself by Augustus John: he started it during the War, but never finished it, and when he died the directors of a company who took over his premises found the portrait and presented it to her. "It has cheered me up no end," she said after she received it.

For a member of the Royal Family living, as it were, on her own and with a diary of engagements now averaging less than two a week, it seems strange, and to some, wrong that she should benefit from the Civil

In December 1982, the Queen Mother opened yet another building named after her – The Queen Mother's Hall at Westfield College, London. But perhaps her visit to the Smithfield Show interested her most. Her heifer, Castle of Mey Eodima, won third prize in the Supreme Fatstock Championship.

duties) go on and off duty in rota, each "shift" lasting from four to six weeks. Between them they keep Clarence House running efficiently both as an administrative enterprise geared to the necessities of the Queen Mother's official life, and as a home, offering her the comforts to which she has become accustomed.

For all that efficiency, she has for many years been indulgently believed to be notoriously unpunctual. This is normally an unforgiveable weakness in any member of the Royal Family, whose schedules are worked out months in advance and usually timed to the minute. Queen Victoria and Queen Mary were both models of punctuality – the latter was even born on the very day she was expected – but the Queen Mother, like Queen Alexandra who was, it is said, late for her own Coronation, tends to let the minutes slip by.

List to the tune of £321,000 per year, almost double Prince Philip's allowance and almost three times those of Princess Anne or Princess Margaret. The answer lies in the Queen Mother's unique rank as widow of a sovereign, which entitles her to a home, a staff and a way of life close to what she would have enjoyed as the King's consort. Consequently, she has a staff of over three dozen – some of whom are on duty part time, and many of whom are unpaid. The unsalaried members of her household are usually old friends holding honorary appointments after many years of faithful service, and her ladies-in-waiting (called Women of the Bedchamber if they attend her on day to day occasions, and Ladies of the Bedchamber if on ceremonial

In late November 1982, the Queen Mother unveiled a plaque on board the Queen Elizabeth 2 (this page) to commemorate that ships involvement in the Falklands War. The link was marked by the inclusion of the Queen Mother's standard at the head of the plaque. (Opposite page, top left) the Queen Mother at the Children of Courage Awards ceremony in December 1982. Here, she gave awards to children who had performed acts of heroism.

What Cecil Beaton had praised as her movements "in slow motion" can evidently have disadvantages. There is a belief that she has a notice on her desk saying in large capital letters DO IT NOW, and an equally widespread counter belief that she has never thought it to have had the slightest effect on her. In effect, any lack of punctuality is more often than not of the type which can always be embraced with cheerfulness,

The Queen Mother, like most other members of her family, makes a point of attending the various ceremonies of remembrance held in November each year. For her in particular, as some of her brothers, nephews and cousins were killed, wounded or taken prisoner in two World Wars, these traditional national commemorations are more than mere ceremonial. (These pages) she always plants a cross in the Royal Legion's Field of Remembrance at St Margaret's Westminster.

namely that which springs from a consuming interest in whom she is meeting, and what she is doing. It is rarely her arrivals that are late – it is the getting away again.

That this tolerable weakness still exists today, when her advanced years if nothing else would give her every excuse for making short work of her official duties, is a measure of the importance she attaches to continuing that work while she has the power to do so. Her few illnesses,

Luxembourg. *The diamond and ruby jewellery provided a contrast with her more functional race-course outfit a few days later, when she visited Kempton Park to see three of her horses in action. Success was moderate – one horse won, one fell and the other was unplaced.*

The Sadler's Wells Foundation was 300 years old in 1983, and the Queen Mother was at the theatre on 22nd February to help them celebrate, where she watched a performance of The Count of

(These pages) the Queen Mother visited the Royal Anglian Regiment in Colchester, in May 1982. Though the inspection of the six guards of honour was accompanied by a sudden squall of rain, the Queen Mother was not put off and continued the parade under an umbrella (left), a gesture which was well received by the regiment.

especially in recent years, have been trivial indeed – the occasional chill and bout of 'flu, the leg ulcer which almost kept her away from the Prince of Wales' wedding in 1981, but which just healed in time, the brief cold which prevented her from joining the rest of her family for the customary Christmas Day Morning Service at St George's Chapel Windsor Castle – all bear satisfactory comparison with those lengthy indispositions which interrupted her honeymoon in 1923, kept her out of action at the time of the death of King George V and again at the Accession of King George VI, or postponed a tour or two in the mid 1960s. Her little brush with the fishbone in November 1982 accentuated her eagerness not to let small matters get in the way of what she clearly enjoys – a job of work which, in its own way and following her own lights, adds to the quality of an all too mundane life today. The "touch of the twinkle which she keeps for old friends" is now a regular accompaniment to even the most ordinary of duties. It is a

trait by which her family have been greatly influenced over the years and which has undoubtedly helped to modernise the monarchy while keeping her young both in spirit and in the esteem of her daughter's subjects. That, in a cynical age when true esteem is hard to come by, is no mean achievement and is ample reward for the long life of dedication, wisdom and inspiration which Queen Elizabeth the Queen Mother has

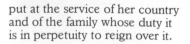

put at the service of her country and of the family whose duty it is in perpetuity to reign over it.

A favourite, deep-turquoise velvet outfit almost matching the Queen Mother's eyes, was seen frequently in 1982, as in February (above, top right and far left) when she visited St Peter's Church, Walworth for a thanksgiving service, and the following month when she opened the Kingston YWCA at Surbiton (left and opposite page).

First published in Great Britain by Colour Library Books Ltd.
© 1983 Illustrations: Keystone Press Agency, London.
© 1983 Text: Colour Library Books, Guildford, Surrey, England.
Display and text filmsetting by Acesetters Ltd., Richmond, Surrey, England.
Printed and bound in Barcelona, Spain.
ISBN 0 86283 116 4